little armoured

For Neecey

little armoured

Rebecca Perry

**Winner of the 2011 *Poetry Wales*
Purple Moose Prize**

SEREN

Seren is the book imprint of
Poetry Wales Press Ltd.
57 Nolton Street, Bridgend, Wales, CF31 3AE
www.seren-books.com

© Rebecca Perry, 2011

ISBN **978-1-85411-621-5**

A CIP record for this title is available from the British Library.

All rights reserved. No part of this publication may be reproduced, stored in a retrieval system, or transmitted at any time or by any means, electronic, mechanical, photocopying, recording or otherwise without the prior permission of the copyright holder.

Printed in Bembo by Berforts Group Limited.

Poetry Wales gratefully acknowledges the sponsorship of Purple Moose Brewery, Porthmadog. **www.purplemoose.co.uk**

Contents

My grandfather considers his life in three stages	7
Namgalsipschlar	9
Libebcnofne	14
Almost but not quite there	15
Other Clouds	16
Wasp	17
Seated Figure of Summer 1573	18
in praise of air rifle shooting instructors	19
What is the most shop-lifted book in the world?	20
Shifting	21
when the wind full of space wears out our faces	22
A Nocturnal	25
The Woman in the Sun, a letter	26
Henry the Navigator, from Sea	27
to provide a definition of piety	28
Up and Up	29
The Pelican	30
The Mice	32
Carapace	34
Surface Level	35
Dinner	36
Hello, Little Bird	37
The Man in the Moon	39
Author Note	40
Acknowledgements	40

My grandfather considers his life in three stages

iii.
Matrimony, two children, some bad things.
He has stood tall and unshaking like the dead apple tree
at the end of his garden. He has forged himself deep –
never moving far; making occasional trips
to local places, the garden, to see family if he has to.
He looks out at the sky from his front room window,
through the net curtains. He says he is waiting
for the mob to come and unceremoniously dismantle him,
pillar by pillar, plucking out the sacred stone
at the centre of his body and smashing it to pieces
against the wall. They will leave one stone to mark the spot.
One stone to stand as the promise of a man that was,
which is better than the reality, he says,
which after all, wasn't so great.

ii.
Posted to Italy, Africa, another place
whose name has now changed. He remembers fires,
and heat even in the dead of night. Everything simmered,
small fires hopped from place to place
like rabbits from hutch to hutch. He never fired a gun.
At night, counted flaming sheep, thought of his wife,
at home, heating the house with coals. He never fired a gun
but people were still dead, scattered around.
He felt, not so much that he was melting but that
perhaps his bones were thinning from the inside out –
He vowed never to leave England again
and never did. This stage ended not with a great fire
or explosion but with a gentle collapse of buckling ash
and a very distinct sense of conceding.

i.
The assembling of himself, piece by piece,
a tiny construction. He has a short film in his mind
of his own creation. He plays it over and over. It is not
a slow process of growth, but his bones coming together
like synchronised swimmers, slotting into place perfectly.
Then, a feeling of strength, being freshly born each day.
Of a good and solid structure – a constant energy,
like tiny bees under his skin. His arms and legs were small,
mighty columns – capable of stopping the sky from falling.
His eyes an excellent brown, like freshly dug earth after rain,
would look directly at the sun, taking everything in.
This stage was short and ended all too suddenly –
washed away like twigs in strong water
one night when he was sleeping, and he woke.

Namgalsipschlar

i. Sodium

My father learnt that Sodium has a boiling point
of ninety seven point seven degrees Celsius

on the same day of summer in the Fifties
Britain gave up the Suez Canal to Egypt.
He liked the notion that people could own water.

The same day his mother lost a baby
and he was told to go outside and play.

Where he sat on the pavement as day darkened,
left to imagine the soft, silvery-white
of that reactive element, that tiny bomb,
stored in a clear tube, hanging like a planet.

ii. Magnesium

On the same day in the Fifties
that John Lennon and Paul McCartney
met for the first time,
reaching for the same glass

and brushing hands,
while Lennon's rock group,
Quarrymen, performed at a church dinner,
my great granddad finally dropped dead.

My father was told to stay put,
which he did,
while the whisky of the deceased
was gathered and smashed in the sink
and a million wrongs cursed over it.

That night, the moon
through the gap in the curtains
was the brilliant white light
of magnesium burning in air,
of electrically ignited flash bulbs,
fireworks and flares.

iii. Aluminium

Stable aluminium
is created when
hydrogen fuses
with magnesium
in either large stars
or in supernovae.

My father read
and repeated,
wrote and repeated
large stars
or supernovae.

iv. Silicon

Elvis Presley released Hound Dog
on my father's birthday.

My father wiped the dust from his mirror
with the back of his hand,

quiffed up his hair with cold water,
forgot about his science books.

Then, for weeks,
You Ain't Never Caught A Rabbit
And You Ain't No Friend Of Mine.

v. Phosphorus

On the day the seasons changed
one day in the Fifties,

my father sat alone
in front of a dying fire –

lit as night fell
to draw the chill from the walls –

my grandmother in hospital
for the second time that year.

He sat alone
and looked as far into the flames

as he felt able to do
without alarming himself

over all the things
he couldn't understand,

watched the fire burn out –
the glow retreating

like an unknown beast
drawing back into a cave.

vi. Sulfur

As my father lay in a bath too hot for the weather
on an unseasonably hot day mid-way through the Fifties,

squeezing the water from a sponge into a bucket at the side,
until he could see a definite difference in the water level

and the little steaming peaks of his knees grew colder
above the surface, losing heat like saucepans with the lids off,

Elvis Presley, The King was bumping into Johnny Cash,
The Man in Black, as he paid a social visit to Sam Phillips.

And the two of them, with Jerry Lee Lewis on piano
started an impromptu jam session with the tapes running.

vii. Chlorine

The pale green paint on the walls
of the Peter Pan Swimming Baths –
faded from brilliant green, to green, to this.

The chlorine; from the Greek, *khlôros*,
meaning pale green, having taken its toll.
The smell of it in the changing rooms
and still on skin and in hair for days after.

My father floating on his back in armbands
looking up at the steel rods in the ceiling's rafters
which would, in exactly twenty four hours,

collapse in on themselves after twenty years
of corrosion. The paper would describe it as
catastrophic; this loss of seven lives
and a much loved community landmark.

viii. Argon

Almost 62 years to the day
Lord Rayleigh and Sir William Ramsay
isolated argon; colourless, odourless, tasteless,
from the Greek meaning 'inactive',
excellent for use in fire extinguishers,
Jackson Pollock died in a car crash aged 44.

69 years exactly to the day
Lord Rayleigh and Sir William Ramsay
isolated argon; the complete octet –
a perfect example of stability,
perfect for culling factory farmed chickens
following the outbreak of disease –
California approved 'Eureka'
as their official state motto.

Libebcnofne

The rain popped clearly on the corrugated iron roof
of a bathroom where a boy who would, one day,
become my father lay watering out the world in a plastic tub.
He mouthed out, soft as corrosion, the word 'Libebcnofne'.
He pressed the tip of his tongue to the back of his teeth
for the 'L' of Lithium, kicked his lips into quick succession
for the Bs of Beryllium and Boron. The back of his throat
blinked for Carbon, his ears hummed for Nnnnnnnitrogen.
Oxygen's O ringed in the air, Flourine's F flew by, and left.
An ear-to-ear smile formed for Neon at a line learnt, to pass on.
He considered how and why ice had formed on the inside
of the window pane, knew the laws of buoyancy by heart,
as his incantations of Archimedes' Principle echoed out with
the rain: *When a body is wholly or partially immersed…*

Almost but not quite there

Running away never amounted to much.
My stuttering feet would not walk
farther than the third lamppost down,
chinking a lunchbox full of china gnomes
chipped from the last time.

My father would take me by the hand
and say, as he inched me nearer home,
sticking your head in the sand
does no one any good,
and where would we be
if we all behaved like ostriches?

Back then everything was as slow
as the setting of ice cubes, slow as the spins
of bakelite telephones,
slow as the sinking of a one-winged wasp in
a paddling pool,

slow as my father's voice singing
a half remembered song about Lahore,
slow as the death of his mate Eddie
who used to drum for Status Quo,
whose handiwork still runs wires
through our house;

slow as the sinking in of his words,
like syrup pressing down into porridge,
after we got tear gassed in Tesco,
that you always need an arm free, an eye open,
a foot to the floor
and darling, remember this,
a tooth you could easily be without.

Other Clouds

```
driving with my father              he said
it is important to see someone die                  to help you understand what life is
to help you understand the things                   you can do to make it easier
when it has to happen to you          he said
maybe it will rain                  it is important to know
the different clouds by sight                       it is important to predict the weather
he said            remember, if you get married
to pick a ring bigger than your finger                      because your fingers,
like your mother's,         swell slightly in the heat
he said            remember we don't
have good knees in this family        you should exercise more
he said            try and think of a philosophy
it is important to know whether       you want to do life carefully
or thought by thought, as it comes                he said
cut down on the adjectives            people have eyes
he said            remember to pick a hot drink
you can order when pressed for time                 don't be the person
holding up the queue                  he said
always wear a watch                   he said
wind down the window a bit            i want to smell the sea
he said            try to eat more fish
if I get all the bones out      would you eat more
he said            i fancy a pint
i'm glad you can hold your drink              he said
are you in fifth gear yet       does that still make you nervous
he said            it wasn't fair
that men used to have to stay outside               when women gave birth
he said men should be allowed         to see life happen
that that is important too            just as much
he said       sometimes he still went to hold my hand
when we crossed the road              he said

he was glad        I never grew taller than him
```

Wasp

little lion. little nibbler.
little face dunker. little duck.
little clinging cashew nut.
little rummager, sifting for gold.
little hovercraft. little clamberer.
little engine. little warrior, little armoured.
little yellow-black armadillo.
little snail-slime wings.
little nuzzler, nuzzling a neck.
little alien, little feeler, little zebra.
little dinosaur legs.
little sycophant. little mounter.
little vampire, little pollen sucking bead.
little pocket knife.

Seated Figure of Summer 1573

I know there is only one way it can go
from here, my sitting spot in the shade
with my back to the sinking sun –

these half peach cheeks will shrink and fall
and my brow of grapes will wrinkle to raisins
for the little birds to peck at in twos and threes.

My parsnip fingers, all heavy and wet
will not be able to pinch their wings
and return them to their branches.

This torso of apples and figs will sink back
and blacken like the opening of a cave –
all my colours gone.

Ants will march into me and carry off
the stalks and pips for a new home, elsewhere,
and I will hollow, hollow, hollow.

My corn cob arms and legs will loosen
and fall away like rotten teeth –
the yellow to brown and all my colours gone.

The pears of my heels will soften with each step.
Small brown patches of mush will give way
and I will fall, here or there,

all my colours gone,
with none of a melting snowman's grace
and some ridiculous final thought.

in praise of air rifle shooting instructors

who stand beside the target
and never flinch
and believe absolutely in your closed eye,

the muscle of your middle finger,
the chip of tongue at the corner of your mouth
who stand in shorts

bearing the still-a-little-pink scars
like constellations on their shins
and believe absolutely it won't happen again.

What is the most shop-lifted book in the world?

How deep is the deepest ocean? I am 6 years old.
Why do cats prefer to die on their own?
How much of the earth's surface is covered in sand?

I have read about it and I think it's deeper than I can go.
How could anyone pull a sword from a stone?
How deep is the deepest ocean? I am 6 years old.

How fast is the Maldives sinking and do the people there know?
How do I know if 'tenanimalsislaminanet' is a palindrome?
How much of the earth's surface is covered in sand?

How long would it take a cherry pip to grow
into a tree? Is it true that diamond is stronger than bone?
How deep is the deepest ocean? I am 6 years old.

How do you know not to pronounce the X in beaux?
How can the library stop you keeping books on loan?
How much of the earth's surface is covered in sand?

How many people can you love in a row?
How can you make sure you don't end up alone?
How deep is the deepest ocean? I am 6 years old.
How much of the earth's surface is covered in sand?

Shifting

All of us crammed in there
like buffalo standing before water at nightfall, looking ahead.
All of us shadows and shapes, quietly shifting.
      That day being your face, and the constant threat of rain –
the air seeming thick as the ground.   Your face
          being the saddest thing I have ever seen.
The weight of our footsteps
            outside the church.
The soft tread of us, our press into the grass;
     temporary craters on soft earth and proof of us being alive –
a dissatisfied herd breathing quietly, waiting to act as one.

when the wind full of space wears out our faces

after Rainer Maria Rilke's *Duino Elegies*

i

breathe your lungs out into the air
maybe the birds will feel the expansion of it.

ii

perhaps the air right now
could only smell this one way
with its billion component parts
and dead skin of the not-living
and fires and weather conditions
and tastes of spices in and out
of our mouths, insides, mouths.

iii

we carry the small fragments of ourselves
like parrots on our shoulders
the socks lined up neat as conkers
the firmly held belief that it is lucky
to be hit in the face by a falling leaf.

iv

we are allowed to cry
in the toilets at work
when someone young dies.

v

i feel as if my body once held two people
and now I am lost inside this stretched out skin
a little deaf, perhaps heartbroken,
walking on, unable to keep out the cold.

vi

we are heroes maybe
we shatter brick walls
then half way through life, we,
with tender mouths,
become someone other.

vii

when there is not enough for us
we will go to the moon
and dig and take. we will gather
up sunlight and bring it back
in drums and boxes and skips.

viii

you boiled down – pen, paper, biscuit –
saying house, fountain, new car,
crack in a cup,
tall grass, fruit-tree, window –
at most: column, tower, castle.

ix

see: the Rider, the Staff, Fruit-Garland
see stars — see both living and being dead,
or the possibility of it.
see Ursa Major, see the one that looks like
a something and then something else again.

x

tell me how good it is
to wake from a bad dream
and have someone there and I will tell you
that things, more often than not
won't work themselves out.

A Nocturnal

after John Donne's *A Nocturnal upon St. Lucie's Day, being the shortest day*

It is the year's midnight and the short day is hers also, Lucy's, who will barely give us a blink of sun. The light has long since died and only hints of it hang in puddles and through the branches of very dark trees.

The early nightfall calls for silence
without even meaning to and we all secretly fear
this darkness might be perpetual. We're urged
to get half an hour of fresh air while there's still light,
take Vitamin D. The sky is an eyelid
we cannot stop closing. The city feels invisible –
our high rise lights and street lights and
fly by nights, not programmed to come on so early,
are little beast eyes waiting to glow in the dark.
The umbrellas from yesterday's heavy rainfall
and fast winds hang crooked and broken
from door handles and the mouths of dustbins.
They are the only bats we have in the city,
or the only ones we allow ourselves to believe in.

The woman in the sun, a letter

I want my feet to tingle with cold again.
I want to be cold with you.
I want you to put your hands between my thighs in bed,
and I would clench them tight for you,
like daisies in a flower press.
I want to press my nipples onto your shoulder blades,
and leave tiny licks of saliva on your back, cold as skis.

I am full of tears.
All day they roll out of my eyes
and fizz to nothing by my feet.
They splash my breasts and for a second it is dark there,
then no. I am dry. I am a pillar of salt.

My body is warmed from the inside out.
My stomach is molten inside my body,
my lungs bubble from the heat of it,
my heart in your hand would be like
taking a potato straight from the oven,
my bones are the wood of a campfire,
my skin is bed sheets slept in for a day and night.

Henry the Navigator, from Sea

I remember wondering
if a willingness to drink someone's spit
means you love them,
lying on the deck, having been sockless
for eight days, hand on chest,
when we first found Cape Verde.

When I am back from here
I would like us to build a new ship.
Your spine should be
the inspiration behind the structure.
It should move over water
in the way your hands move.
I will call it, perhaps, Salgado,
because of the way
your skin sometimes tastes of salt,
which is a thing I never tell you.

to provide a definition of piety

Apollo has ideas about love.
        You should watch your lover on the toilet, at least once.
        You should be happy to share bathwater.
Sometimes his ideas are accompanied by music and the gods
hold one another and shake,
        if you think something you should say it aloud immediately.
        You should never feel nervous when your lover holds scissors.
Sometimes he recites his ideas in verse and the gods
fall in love with the god next to them,
        be willing to put any part of their body in your mouth
        look impressed if they write you a song.
Sometimes he whispers his ideas, naked, and the gods
lie down on sheets and kiss each other's necks
and bite lips and pull hair and moan.
        Apollo has responsibilities.
He sees Hephaestus sitting apart from them
with his poor legs stretched out, muscles like soft plums,
        Apollo feels bad when things go so wrong.
trying to make flames big enough to show Aphrodite
that she should love him, while she leans away
        Apollo feels bad when vultures triumph over gentler things
her chin on Ares' shoulder, fingers moving,
nipples flashing pink and gold in the firelight.

Up and Up

If I have to die now
at least I can die
while there is an airplane above me
and its lights are blinking
slow and steady as my pulse,
and there are people asleep inside it
playing with their toes.

At least I can see some stars,
even here – the sky is so dark
and the only cloud looks like an x-ray
of a tibia; creaseless, like scaffold.

If I do have to die now
at least it isn't as cold as it could be
and I have gloves on, even.
I haven't met anyone I want to marry
and the ground is hard, clean enough.
The air is doing nothing
so the bare trees look like
frozen fireworks, or veins,
or horses leaping into one another,
reckless, magnificent.

The Pelican

struts
through the small crowd

that parts
like a biblical sea

and then stands
still as still to watch
this great nameless thing

that holds
the entire concept
of possibility in its beak,

that doesn't acknowledge a soul
as it walks
to the tip of the land,

it is purposeful, solid – imagine
how it becomes a small white boat
on the water surface

where it
turns back to the crowd,
still parted,

still silent, who can see, now,
the new swell of water in its beak
puffed and taut and terrifying,

the light of the huge sun shining
through it like a water balloon,
and the parted crowd gasps at this,

this feat of nature and
the absolute disregard
for proportion.

The Mice

They are eating it —
the poison we have left down for them.

There are bite marks around the edges
and, sometimes, the blocks move

a few centimetres overnight.
We hear them now and then,

rifling through our bag of plastic bags.
We see them dart, little shadows,

across the floor or kitchen counter.
Then, yesterday, it all stopped.

The poison did not move overnight
and we heard nothing

and saw nothing
and we knew that, for now,

it was over.
That they were behind the walls

and skirting boards; quiet, still,
nestled all together like toys

in the window of a toy shop,
in an imaginary world,

in a children's picture book –
one of them destined to come to life

when the lights are turned off
and the human world sleeps.

Carapace

Quietly sitting, me.
Tiny by the stove,
my not-quite Great-Aunt
is heating up beans.
Eyes in the back of her head.

She has smoked in this house
for forty solid years,
stinging eyes, staining carpets
and curtains, all yellow.
In winter the burning smell

of the electric heater
humming like a bee in the corner
of the room, its orangeness
brighter than your eyes expect.
In summer one door open for air.

The tortoise, named after
her husband who died at thirty,
missing its two back legs
pulls itself along the carpet
like a soldier, proud of itself

almost, little mouth fixed in place,
eyes heavy with the weight of
I can't imagine what,
a box of matches balanced
on top of its shell.

Surface Level

On nights like this it can be hard to sit still.
It can be hard to make human contact when
we sweat as instantly as thunderstorms.
The air all bog cotton and centre of a cloud,
rouses itself into formation, rolls up, gathers.
The windows are blank eyes, black and still.
The windows are gaping mouths and no air.
We lie out flat on sheetless beds, cold floors;
limbs limp like foxes' at the hems of country lanes.

Outside, the frogs who tried to cross the road
dot the tarmac in their hapless constellation,
freckle-flat, browning rapidly like apple bites.
The sky cracks open, sudden as light. We watch
the downpour, its coax; the rain is swelling them up.

Dinner

The worst part of it all
is watching you de-bone a fish.

The head is off in the blink of any eye,
stone grey, poor headless subject now

and you are a fat king having your way
with a fork and a spoon.

The tail the same; the motor, propeller
of probably an impressive distance

that would surprise us if we knew,
and that too is pinchpulled off

with a wrinkle of your nose.
The skin is split, scales are scraped –

pulled back like curtains to a show
I don't want to see. The spine,

the fine rack of bones is eased out
with the care we take to hold babies,

and sideplated beside two lemon quarters.
Stripped of finery, de-robed, it is dinner.

I pick up the comb and hold it to the window,
the bones buzz with the light of it.

Hello, Little Bird

For X

You hate that the sun is always out,
even when it rains,
and all you want is to be cold.

It is like a bee behind a curtain
that won't fly out of the window,
won't get out of the room.

You say that sometimes
you wish the sun would fuck off and die,
then feel bad for wishing that.

If I tell you it's raining here,
you ask how much rain. You see snow
on the news and it makes you sad.

You have started taking pictures
on plastic Holgas cameras, with film reel –
digital photos seem dishonest to you.

They can't capture the sun's buzz,
the bougainvillea across your sister's face –
two exposures, of two lovely things.

You send me a picture of a rubber duck
on a windowsill – one perfect half
of bright orange beak, bright yellow body

and the other half bleached almost grey.
You say the sun is a big tongue;
it is licking the flavour from everything.

You say a boy you went to school with
jumped from a roof, and that heroin
feels like a ghost no one will believe in,

even though it is moving things
in front of your eyes, and throwing knives
across the kitchen.

You haven't worn socks
since you left here and you miss the feelings
of wet feet and puddles and rubber soles.

You send me a picture
of the view from your window
and your room, from the doorway.

You send me a picture
of you in a boat, holding a line.
Turns out I am a terrible fisherman. I don't mind.

I send you a picture
of the sign in Vauxhall you loved so much
Tethered balloon ride, 500 metres.

You will come here again in Spring.
You ask if you can take photos of me
in the prime of my life.

The Man in the Moon

The man in the moon is lonely. There are only so many
times you can eat alone and wow at the view over wine,
there are only so many nights you can clap a shooting star
and hear your clap crack out into the yawning air
and away from you like footsteps going down stairs.
There's only a certain number of one-man dances;
you need two for the Samba, Kazatzka, Cha Cha.
A line dance needs a line, as does the Conga.
Sometimes he'll do the Funky Chicken or bop along
to a Festival Automne and love how lively France is.

There are only so many slow somersaults you can do
before the blood fills your head like sand in an egg timer,
before Earth starts to look the same from every angle;
the Nile and Parana get in a tangle and there's no longer
a blind bit of difference between Australia and Greenland.
Before the equator could just as well split the world
like an apple; stalk to bottom, past the pips, through the core.
There are only so many frames to dust, pillows to fluff,
pens to shuffle – things that can be arranged, rearranged
and arranged again to just the way he likes them.

Author note

Rebecca Perry was born in London in 1986. She graduated from the Centre for New Writing at The University of Manchester in 2008 with a master's degree in Creative Writing and now lives and works back in London.

Rebecca has had work recently published in *Iota, Smiths Knoll, The Manchester Review* and *The Rialto*. She placed third in the 2010 Plough Prize, and was Highly Commended in the 2011 Bridport Prize. Rebecca has also contributed to *This Line is Not for Turning: An Anthology of Contemporary British Prose Poetry* (Cinnamon Press).

Acknowledgments

I would like to acknowledge and thank *Ambit, Ampersand Review, The Frogmore Papers, Iota, Magma, New Welsh Review, Orbis, Poetry Wales, Smiths Knoll, The Manchester Review* and the *Rialto*, for publishing many of these poems prior to their appearance in this collection.

I would also like to express my gratitude to Zoë Skoulding for her assistance in putting this pamphlet together.

Finally, a special thank you to John McAuliffe – a brilliant poet and mentor – to whom I owe a great deal.